MY STORY
BY RAMON CASTRO MARIN

The Startup Shortcut

THE FUTURE IS HERE, AND IT'S TIME TO BUILD.

The Startup Shortcut by Ramon Castro

Chapter 1: The Seed of Ambition

The flickering glow of the CRT monitor cast an almost hypnotic blue light across my ten-year-old face. My thumbs flew across the keyboard, fingers instinctively navigating the familiar terrain of the virtual battlefield. It wasn't just a game; it was a competition, a test of strategy and reflexes that demanded complete focus. Victory wasn't just about bragging rights among friends, it was a personal triumph, a validation of my growing obsession – esports.

Even at that young age, the burgeoning world of competitive video games sparked something within me. It wasn't just the thrill of competition, though that certainly played a part. It was the intricate planning, the team coordination, the constant evolution of the meta-game that captivated me. Witnessing the rise of professional players, the burgeoning tournaments with passionate crowds, I knew I wasn't just witnessing a trend; I was witnessing the birth of something monumental.

My bedroom wasn't just a refuge anymore, it was a training ground. Hours were spent honing my skills, devouring online forums for strategy guides, and studying the tactics employed by the pros. This wasn't just a casual hobby; it was the seed of an ambition beginning to take root. The dream of becoming a part of this electrifying world, not just as a player, but as someone who could shape it, fueled my relentless pursuit of knowledge.

But the world outside my bedroom window seemed oblivious to the revolution brewing online. Esports was still a niche

The Startup Shortcut by Ramon Castro

interest, scoffed at by some and dismissed as a passing fad by others. Yet, the conviction within me only grew stronger. I knew, with unwavering certainty, that this wasn't a passing fancy; it was the future. And I, a wide-eyed kid armed with nothing but a keyboard and a burning ambition, was determined to be a part of it.

Years of honing my skills and devouring every scrap of esports knowledge culminated in the moment I stepped onto the stage. The Costa Rican National Esports League (CRNEL) was the first major tournament in my home country, and the energy was electric. Thousands of spectators, fueled by adrenaline and team loyalty, filled the venue. The roar of the crowd washed over me as I took my place at the designated computer, my heart hammering a frantic rhythm against my ribs.

Hype Holdings, the team I'd meticulously built with a handful of like-minded individuals, had become a reality. We weren't just a bunch of kids playing games in our bedrooms anymore; we were a force to be reckoned with. The months leading up to this event were a blur of intense practice sessions, late-night strategy discussions, and the ever-present gnawing pressure of expectation.

We had poured everything we had into this competition. We meticulously analyzed the competition, identified potential weaknesses, and honed our own strategies to a razor's edge. There was a palpable tension in the air, a mix of nerves and exhilaration, as we awaited the first match. Everything we'd worked for, all the countless hours of practice, came down to these moments under the unforgiving glare of the spotlight.

The Startup Shortcut by Ramon Castro

The competition itself was a whirlwind of intense concentration and calculated plays. Our months of preparation paid off.We moved with a practiced efficiency, our teamwork honed to near-telepathic levels. Each victory sent a surge of adrenaline through us, fueled the roaring cheers of the crowd. But we couldn't afford complacency. Every opponent was a challenge, every victory a stepping stone towards the ultimate goal – claiming the CRNEL championship.

In its first attempt Hype Holdings, the scrappy team from a small Central American nation, had conquered the Costa Rican National Esports League with a score unheard of in the world of esports, 21-0. That victory felt like the culmination of a lifetime's work, a testament to our dedication and unwavering belief.

The CRNEL win propelled us onto the international stage. Invitations poured in, and soon Hype Holdings found ourselves competing in the World Esports Federation (WEF) in Los Angeles. The competition was fierce; we were facing the best teams from across the globe. But fueled by our recent victory and a relentless hunger to prove ourselves, we held our own.

The Startup Shortcut by Ramon Castro

Chapter 2: The Higher you Climb, the Harder the Fall.

After two very successful years of operating, the cracks in Hype Holdings' foundation began to show subtly at first. Losses that were once anomalies became more frequent. Sponsors, initially enamored with our winning streak, began to express concerns. Our once-unified team dynamic fractured under the pressure. Arguments erupted during practice sessions, strategies became muddled, and individual egos clashed.

I, consumed by the external trappings of success, failed to recognize the storm brewing within my own team. Instead of addressing these issues head-on, I clung to the hope that our past victories were enough. It was a grave mistake. The WEF that year ended in a disappointing showing, a stark reminder of our decline.
By 2022, the cracks had become chasms. Sponsors pulled out, morale plummeted, and talented players sought opportunities elsewhere. The team I had poured my heart and soul into began to crumble. Despite a desperate attempt to salvage the situation, the inevitable finally arrived. Hype Holdings was forced to shut down, a cautionary tale of a meteoric rise undone by the pitfalls of unchecked ambition.

The sting of that failure was a bitter pill to swallow. But amidst the ashes of Hype Holdings, a seed of a different kind began to germinate – the seed of self-awareness and a burning desire to learn from my mistakes. The story of Hype Holdings may have ended, but my journey in the world of

The Startup Shortcut by Ramon Castro

esports was far from over. The lessons learned, however harsh, would become the foundation for a new venture, one built on a more solid foundation, one destined to avoid the pitfalls that had brought Hype crashing down.

The aftermath of Hype Holdings' collapse left a hollow ache in my gut. The once vibrant energy that had consumed my life had been replaced by a heavy silence. Yet, amidst the disappointment, a strange clarity began to emerge. The months following the company's closure were a period of introspection, a time for me to dissect the reasons behind our failure.

It wasn't just about the mistakes made on the strategic or team management side. As I delved deeper, my focus began to shift towards the business side of esports. The industry, once dominated by a passionate amateur spirit, was rapidly changing. Investors were pouring in, vying for a piece of this burgeoning market. Traditional sporting giants were taking notice, establishing their own esports teams and leagues. This influx of capital exposed a critical weakness: a fragmented industry landscape.

Numerous esports organizations, each with its own game focus and regional presence, jostled for sponsorships, media attention, and a slice of the growing fan base. This disorganization, I realized, wasn't just inefficient; it hampered the long-term growth of the entire industry. Sponsors faced a logistical nightmare when trying to reach a global audience, fans were bombarded with a confusing array of leagues and teams, and the professional infrastructure needed to truly legitimize esports lagged behind.

Here, amidst the chaos, I saw an opportunity. Not just to redeem myself from the ashes of Hype Holdings, but to contribute to the future of esports in a way I hadn't envisioned before. The fragmented industry, once a source of frustration for sponsors and fans alike, presented a compelling proposition – consolidation. By merging the best and brightest of these organizations, I could create a unified esports powerhouse, a single entity capable of attracting top-tier sponsors, solidifying the professional infrastructure, and ultimately propelling esports into the mainstream.

This vision, ambitious yet audacious, became the driving force behind my next chapter. The thrill of competition on the virtual battlefield may have subsided, but a different kind of fire ignited within me – the fire of an entrepreneur with a vision to reshape the future of esports.

The idea for E-America Capital wasn't born in a flash of brilliance; it was meticulously crafted over countless cups of coffee and late-night brainstorming sessions. I devoured industry reports, analyzing the strengths and weaknesses of various esports organizations. I reached out to former competitors, industry insiders, and even potential investors, gauging their interest in a unified front.

The biggest challenge lay in overcoming the skepticism. Many esports organizations prided themselves on their independence, fiercely loyal to their regional roots and specific gaming focus. Merging these disparate entities into a cohesive whole seemed like a near-impossible feat.

The Startup Shortcut by Ramon Castro

But I had an ace up my sleeve. My experience with Hype Holdings, while ultimately a failure, had equipped me with invaluable knowledge of the industry and its players. I understood the frustrations of sponsors and fans, the inefficiencies of the fragmented landscape. More importantly, I understood the passion that burned within these organizations, the dedication of the teams and their fan bases.

Thus, E-America Capital wasn't simply a financial proposition; it was a vision for a brighter future of esports. We wouldn't just be acquiring companies, we would be forging partnerships, building a unified front that could elevate the entire industry. My pitch focused on leveraging combined resources to attract top-tier sponsors, investing in infrastructure and professional development for players, and ultimately securing esports' rightful place alongside traditional sports on the global stage.

The initial reception was, as expected, mixed. Some saw it as a blatant power grab, a way for me to control the industry.Others remained skeptical, unsure of the proposed benefits of unification. But slowly, through persistence and a genuine passion for esports, the tide began to turn. The potential benefits, particularly the prospect of attracting major sponsors and a more sustainable future, resonated with a growing number of organizations.

With each partnership secured, E-America Capital's foundation grew stronger. What began as a bold vision on a whiteboard was slowly transforming into a reality, a financial juggernaut poised to reshape the esports landscape. The seeds of a new future were being sown, but the path to dominance wouldn't be without its thorns. The challenge of merging these once-independent entities awaited, and the very passion that fueled the industry could also be its biggest obstacle.

The Startup Shortcut by Ramon Castro

Chapter 3: Resistance and Resurgence

The road to esports unification wasn't paved with rose petals. E-America Capital's initial foray into the market was met with a wave of resistance, a fierce pushback from those who viewed our vision as a Trojan horse, a veiled attempt at establishing a monopoly. Here were the very organizations I hoped to partner with, the passionate teams that fueled the industry's spirit, raising their shields in defiance.
The arguments were fierce. Accusations of corporate greed and stifling independent voices echoed through the esports community. Some worried about the homogenization of the industry, the loss of regional identities and unique league formats. Others, particularly players from smaller organizations, feared being swallowed by a behemoth and losing their competitive edge.

The media gleefully picked up on the narrative, painting E-America Capital as the villain, the ruthless conglomerate threatening to devour the vibrant soul of esports. Sponsors, ever wary of controversy, took a wait-and-see approach,hesitant to back a company embroiled in such volatile public discourse.
The initial months were a brutal test of resolve. Every potential partnership felt like an uphill battle.

We faced a constant barrage of criticism, questioned at every turn. Doubt began to gnaw at the edges of my conviction. Had I misinterpreted the needs of the industry? Was the dream of a unified esports a utopian fallacy?

The Startup Shortcut by Ramon Castro

Then, in late 2019, a storm unlike any other began to brew on the horizon. The world watched in disbelief as the COVID-19 pandemic swept across the globe. Traditional sporting events were canceled, stadiums lay eerily empty. Suddenly, the once-fragmented world of esports found itself thrust into the spotlight.

This was the moment the tide began to turn. With traditional sports sidelined, esports emerged as a beacon of normalcy, a source of entertainment and competition for a world on lockdown. However, the fragmented nature of the industry, the very thing we'd been advocating against, became a crippling disadvantage.

Sponsors, desperate for content and a captive audience, found it difficult to navigate the labyrinth of leagues and teams.The lack of a unified infrastructure – broadcast rights, standardized production value – hampered esports' ability to capitalize on this golden opportunity.

The esports winter brought about by the pandemic proved to be a turning point, but it wasn't just about highlighting the industry's vulnerabilities. It also opened a door of opportunity, and through that door stepped a key commercial ally – Epic Games. The creators of the global phenomenon, Fortnite, Epic recognized the potential of esports during this crisis.However, they too faced the frustration of navigating a fragmented landscape.

Discussions with Epic Games were a masterclass in commercial pragmatism. While they shared our vision for a unified esports scene, their approach was refreshingly blunt.

The Startup Shortcut by Ramon Castro

They weren't driven by altruism; they saw an opportunity to leverage a consolidated industry to maximize the reach and profitability of their flagship title.

It was a harsh lesson in the realities of the business world. As much as esports was driven by passion and community, it was also a multi-billion dollar industry, and the stakes were high. Epic's involvement wasn't an act of charity; it was a strategic move. Yet, despite the pragmatism, it was a partnership that resonated deeply.

Epic's support, coupled with the stark realities exposed by the pandemic, began to shift the narrative. Organizations that were once staunchly opposed to consolidation started to see the merit in a unified front. The dream of a global esports stage, once ridiculed as a power grab, now seemed like a lifeline thrown during a desperate time.

The brutal resistance we initially faced hadn't been without its lessons. It forced us to refine our pitch, to demonstrate a deep understanding of the concerns of individual organizations. We learned the importance of collaboration, of building partnerships that went beyond financial incentives. Ultimately, it wasn't just about acquiring companies; it was about creating a shared vision, a win-win scenario for all stakeholders.

The esports winter, a period of forced hibernation due to the pandemic, ultimately served as a catalyst for a rapid thaw. With Epic Games joining the fray and the industry's vulnerabilities laid bare, E-America Capital found itself at the forefront of a resurgent esports scene. The tide of resistance began to recede, replaced by a wave of cautious optimism.Organizations, once fiercely independent, recognized the need for a unified voice, a single entity capable of navigating the complexities of the global stage.

This newfound openness allowed E-America Capital to forge critical partnerships. We weren't just acquiring companies; we were strategically integrating them, leveraging their strengths and expertise to build a robust esports ecosystem.Broadcast rights were consolidated, ensuring high-quality productions that rivaled traditional sports. Standardized player contracts and league formats were established, fostering stability and professionalism.

The culmination of these efforts came in the form of the Global Esports Federation (GEF). This wasn't just a symbolic gesture; it was a concrete manifestation of a unified industry. The GEF served as the governing body, overseeing regulations, player welfare initiatives, and international competitions. E-America Capital, once seen as a potential monopolizing force, became a cornerstone of this new organization, utilizing its financial muscle and industry knowledge to propel the GEF forward.

The recovery of esports was swift and dramatic. Sponsors, now faced with a streamlined and professional esports landscape, poured back in, eager to capitalize on the industry's surging popularity. Broadcast deals were secured with major networks, bringing esports into living rooms around the world. Fan engagement soared, fueled by high-production-value competitions and a unified global narrative.

The Startup Shortcut by Ramon Castro

The esports winter, a period of immense challenge, had ultimately paved the way for a golden age. What was once a fragmented collection of passionate teams had transformed into a well-oiled machine, a global entertainment powerhouse. However, the journey wasn't without its scars. The initial resistance, while overcome, served as a constant reminder of the delicate balance between passion and pragmatism in the world of esports. The future, filled with promise and brimming with potential, still held challenges – maintaining the core values of esports while navigating the ever-evolving commercial landscape. But for now, as I stood at the helm of a unified industry, the bittersweet satisfaction of redemption mingled with the exhilarating anticipation of the road ahead.

The Startup Shortcut by Ramon Castro

Chapter 4: The Allure of Innovation

Having witnessed the transformative power of consolidation in the esports arena, I couldn't help but be captivated by its potential application in other industries. The concept, often attributed to the legendary banker J.P. Morgan, was a familiar refrain – "morganization," the strategic acquisition and merging of competing entities to create a dominant force. While E-America Capital's success in esports had been a testament to this strategy, I was determined to explore its applicability beyond the world of competitive gaming.

My next venture, E-Pay, emerged from an observation on the increasingly complex landscape of payment systems. The industry, like esports in its early days, was fragmented. A plethora of digital wallets, credit card networks, and regional payment processors jostled for dominance, creating a confusing and often inefficient experience for consumers and businesses alike.

E-Pay, I envisioned, would become the ultimate digital wallet, a singular platform that would revolutionize the way transactions were conducted. Fueled by the success of E-America Capital, I embarked on an ambitious plan – the morganization of the payment system industry. We began acquiring prominent players, merging their technologies and customer bases under the E-Pay umbrella.

The initial steps were exhilarating. Just as with E-America Capital, the consolidation seemingly offered numerous benefits. Consumers would have a single platform to manage all their transactions, businesses would enjoy a wider reach and streamlined operations, and E-Pay, positioned as the central hub, would hold immense power and influence.

However, unlike the esports industry, which thrived on a shared passion for competitive gaming, the world of payments was a different beast. Here, competition wasn't just about winning tournaments; it was about innovation, flexibility, and the ability to cater to specific regional needs and regulations. The very essence of what made E-Pay a potential powerhouse – its centralized nature – became its Achilles' heel.

The initial euphoria surrounding E-Pay quickly dissipated as we encountered the harsh realities of the payments landscape. Consumers, accustomed to established payment methods and wary of entrusting all their financial transactions to a single entity, were hesitant to migrate to E-Pay. Businesses, too, expressed concerns about the potential for monopolistic practices and a lack of flexibility in a rapidly evolving industry.

The failure of E-Pay's initial morganization strategy was a bitter pill to swallow. However, amidst the disappointment, a crucial realization dawned. The world of finance, particularly within the burgeoning realm of digital transactions, wasn't seeking a centralized behemoth. It craved innovation, a system that could leverage the power of technology to create a more secure, efficient, and decentralized future.
This revelation was the catalyst for a pivotal shift. Instead of clinging to the failing morganization strategy, we pivoted, a skill I had honed during the early days of Hype Holdings. E-Pay wouldn't become a one-stop shop for all financial

transactions; it would become a bridge, a gateway to the exciting world of Decentralized Finance (DeFi).

The concept was revolutionary. DeFi aimed to eliminate the need for centralized institutions like banks, fostering a peer-to-peer financial system powered by blockchain technology. E-Pay, instead of trying to dominate the traditional payment landscape, would position itself as a user-friendly platform facilitating seamless interaction with this new financial frontier.
The pivot wasn't without its challenges. Understanding the intricacies of blockchain technology and navigating the volatile world of cryptocurrency required a steep learning curve. However, the potential rewards were immense. By embracing the decentralized future of finance, E-Pay could carve out a valuable niche, a trusted companion guiding users through this uncharted territory.

The road ahead wouldn't be easy. The cryptocurrency market was rife with volatility and regulatory uncertainties. But this time, E-Pay wouldn't be an outsider forcing its way in. We would become a part of this nascent ecosystem, a collaborator and innovator driving the future of decentralized finance. The colossal dream of a single, centralized E-Pay may have died, but in its wake, a far more exciting opportunity had emerged.

The relaunch of E-Pay wasn't a flashy media blitz or a splashy marketing campaign. Instead, we adopted a more measured approach, focusing on building trust and establishing ourselves as a reliable guide to the world of DeFi. Partnering with the Incova Group, led by the visionary

Mr. Yassir Vargas, proved to be a pivotal step in this endeavor.

The Incova Group, brought a wealth of expertise and a deep understanding of the regulatory landscape surrounding cryptocurrency. Mr. Vargas, a respected figure in the industrial world, became a valuable advisor, his guidance instrumental in navigating the complexities of DeFi.

Together, we meticulously crafted E-Pay 2.0. This wasn't just a digital wallet; it was an educational platform, a user-friendly interface that demystified the world of blockchain technology and cryptocurrency. Our focus shifted from transaction dominance to user empowerment. We offered educational resources, explainer videos, and a dedicated customer support team equipped to answer any questions, big or small.

The initial response was cautious but positive. Tech-savvy early adopters were drawn to the platform's user-friendliness and its commitment to education. Slowly, a community began to form, a network of individuals eager to explore the potential of DeFi. E-Pay, no longer a competitor, became a collaborator, fostering connections between users and leading DeFi projects.

The growth of E-Pay wasn't meteoric; it was organic. Word-of-mouth recommendations and positive reviews from early adopters fueled our expansion. As the DeFi ecosystem matured, E-Pay became an indispensable tool, a trusted gateway for users to navigate this exciting new frontier. Partnerships with established cryptocurrency exchanges and leading DeFi protocols further solidified our position as a vital bridge between traditional finance and the decentralized future.

While E-America Capital would always hold a special place as the company that revolutionized esports, E-Pay's success mirrored a different kind of victory. It was a testament to our ability to adapt, to learn from our mistakes and pivot in the face of unforeseen challenges. E-Pay, born from the ashes of a failed attempt at centralization, had become a shining example of innovation within the rapidly evolving world of decentralized finance. It became, in its own right, the second jewel in the crown of my entrepreneurial journey.

The story of E-Pay wasn't just about financial success; it was a testament to the power of embracing change and the importance of collaborating within a dynamic ecosystem. And as I looked towards the future, I knew that this ability to adapt, to learn, and to evolve would be the key to navigating the ever-changing landscape of the business world. For an entrepreneur, the journey is never truly over; it's a continuous process of exploration, innovation, and, at times, reinvention. And with each new challenge, each unexpected turn, the thrill of the chase, the fire of that initial spark that ignited my passion for esports, continued to burn brightly.

Chapter 5: The Birth of E-Corp

Gazing out at the bustling cityscape from my office window, a sense of accomplishment washed over me. E-America Capital and E-Pay, two seemingly disparate ventures, had carved their own unique paths, each contributing significantly to my journey as an entrepreneur. Yet, a nagging feeling persisted, a sense that something was missing.

Both esports and decentralized finance were booming industries, each on the precipice of a global explosion. E-America Capital had established a robust infrastructure for esports, while E-Pay provided a user-friendly gateway to the exciting world of DeFi. However, there was a disconnect, a missed opportunity to truly leverage the synergies between these two revolutionary forces.

This realization became the genesis of E-Corp. It wasn't just another company; it was a culmination, an ambitious vision to create a single entity that would bridge the gap between esports, decentralized finance, and the global financial stage. E-Corp would be the intersection of my ventures, a powerhouse poised to reshape the financial landscape of the ever-evolving world of esports.

Imagine a future where passionate esports fans could not only cheer for their favorite teams but also directly invest in their success. A future where esports organizations could leverage cutting-edge financial tools to secure funding, manage player contracts, and reward their loyal fanbases. E-Corp, powered by the combined expertise of E-America Capital and E-Pay, aimed to make this vision a reality.

The Startup Shortcut by Ramon Castro

The possibilities were endless. E-Corp could offer a range of innovative financial products and services tailored specifically for the esports ecosystem. Tokenized fan engagement platforms could allow fans to purchase fractional ownership of their favorite teams, directly impacting their fortunes. Decentralized finance solutions could streamline player transactions and provide esports organizations with greater financial flexibility.

But the impact wouldn't be limited to esports. By creating a bridge between the passionate world of gaming and the sophisticated realm of finance, E-Corp aimed to open up the global financial stage to a whole new generation of investors.It was a way to democratize finance, to offer esports fans an opportunity to participate in a previously inaccessible market.

The road ahead wouldn't be without its challenges. Regulatory hurdles surrounding cryptocurrency and the ever-evolving nature of esports itself presented formidable obstacles. But for me, the potential rewards outweighed the risks. E-Corp wasn't just about financial gain; it was about creating a sustainable future for the industry I loved, a future where esports wasn't just a spectator sport, but a dynamic ecosystem where fans and players alike could be active participants in its financial success.

The creation of E-Corp marked a pivotal point in my entrepreneurial journey. It wasn't just the culmination of past successes; it was a springboard into a future brimming with possibilities. The convergence of esports, decentralized finance, and the ever-evolving technological landscape promised a future more exciting than anything I could have imagined at the outset.

On the horizon, the concept of the Metaverse loomed large. This immersive virtual world, powered by advancements in artificial intelligence and virtual reality, promised to revolutionize the way we interact with the digital world. Esports,already a leader in pushing the boundaries of virtual competition, stood to be at the forefront of this digital revolution.

Imagine a future where esports tournaments take place in meticulously crafted virtual arenas, blurring the lines between reality and simulation. Fans, equipped with VR headsets, wouldn't just be watching games; they'd be experiencing them,immersed in the roar of the crowd and the heat of the competition. E-Corp, with its established infrastructure in esports and its expertise in digital financial tools, could be at the forefront of shaping this metaverse esports experience.

The role of AI would also be transformative. Imagine intelligent training programs that analyze player performance with unparalleled precision, crafting personalized strategies to optimize every move. Or consider AI-powered commentators delivering real-time insights and analysis, enriching the viewing experience for fans across the globe. E-Corp, by embracing AI and its applications within the esports ecosystem, could unlock a new era of competitive excellence and fan engagement.

As I look towards the future, a sense of exhilaration mingles with the responsibility that comes with being at the forefront of groundbreaking change. The esports industry, once a niche passion project, stands poised to become a cultural phenomenon, a global entertainment powerhouse fueled by cutting-edge technology and innovative financial solutions. E-Corp, as the bridge between these worlds, has the potential to be a vital player in this exciting new era.

This book is not just about my journey; it's an invitation to be a part of this ongoing story. The future of esports, fueled by the Metaverse, AI, and decentralized finance, is being written as we speak. And with E-Corp as your guide, you too can have a front-row seat to the most exhilarating chapter yet. The future is here, and it's time to play.

About the Author

Ramon Castro Marin is a Costa Rican businessman and influencer. He currently serves as Chairman and CEO of E-Corp Global Holdings, a prominent company in technological infrastructure and media. He is a leading entrepreneur in the Esports, Digital Payments and Information Technology industries as well as a prominent speaker at multiple industry events.

www.ingramcontent.com/pod-product-compliance
Lightning Source LLC
Chambersburg PA
CBHW071223240526
45470CB00018B/2296